MISSIONARY TRAINING GUIDE

14 Things You Should Know Before You Go!

Rafielle E. Usher, M.A.

Foreword by Rev. Anthony Dodd, M.A.

Second Edition

© O.M.I. International 2011

Published by O.M.I. International
13245 Atlantic Blvd., Ste. 4-233
Jacksonville Fl. 32225

Visit our website for more information:

www.omiinternational.org

Table of Contents

Missions in the 21st Century

By Rev. Anthony Dodd, M.Div., Church of God

All throughout the world people are in desperate spiritual, emotional, and financial need. These lost souls are crying out for help. They need compassionate people to come and bring them good news and helping hands. As representatives of Christ, we are the voice of this generation who must respond to these cries with "Lord, here am I, send me!"

The mission of God, *Missio Dei*, is to bring hope to those who have no hope. When Jesus came to earth, he focused much of his ministry on those who were poor, social outcasts, and demon oppressed. Throughout history and especially in the 21st century, poverty, societal woes, and the corruption of governments have kept many people around the world bound in chains of affliction. God knows of their suffering and hears their cries for help.

As we sit in our churches on Sunday morning, we rejoice in the fact that Jesus Christ came to set the captives free and minister healing to the brokenhearted. However, have we truly allowed our hearts to be moved with compassion to be the ones who carry out God's mission in the 21st century? God is still speaking to us today and the Spirit says, "Go therefore and make disciples of all the nations, baptizing them in the name of the Father and of the Son and of the Holy Spirit, teaching them to observe all things that I have commanded you; and lo, I am with you always, even to the end of the age" (Matthew 28:19-20, NKJV).

God's mission is one that is Spirit inspired. Consider the story in the book of Acts where Paul experienced a vision from the Holy Spirit in which a man cried out to him and said, "Come over to Macedonia, and help us" (Acts 16: 9). After conferring with the others with him, Paul and his fellow workers immediately set sail for Macedonia. Within only a short time, Lydia and her household were saved upon hearing the gospel, and a slave girl possessed with a spirit of divination was delivered from the evil spirit. It is interesting that Lydia, a seller of purple, was a worshipper of God, but God had to open Lydia's heart to the gospel in order for her household to be saved (Acts 16: 14).

We can surmise from this whole account that God had heard Lydia's prayers and even those of the slave girl who cried out to Paul and his companions saying, "These men are the servants of the Most High God, who proclaim to us the way of salvation" (Acts 16: 17). In a sense, Lydia's prayers and the slave girl's cries are echoed through the man as he cries out to Paul in the vision given to him by the Holy Spirit.

If we as servants of the Most High God want to join in God's mission to save the lost, we must pray that our spiritual ears will be opened to hear the voice of the Spirit and that the cries of people around the world who are in great need will move our hearts with compassion. Proverbs 29:18 says, "Where there is no vision, the people perish." The Hebrew word for vision in this verse is *chazown*. According to Strong's Concordance (H2377), it is a "vision (in ecstatic state)," "vision (in night)," or an "oracle, prophecy (divine communication)." Paul heard God's voice (divine communication) through his nightly vision. We must be open to hearing God's voice in order that we might hear the cries of the people around the world and be God's representatives and spokespersons for missions in the 21st century.

Chapter One:

Recognizing The Call To Missions

The call to missions is when God speaks to a person's heart about serving in a land or with a people group that is not his or her own. When God speaks, it is important to recognize that He is not confined to using only words to communicate His call. God may speak using physical images, visions, or dreams, or simply by giving a person a passion for or an interest in a people group, land, or country. Even then, God is not confined to such methods. He can use any creative method that He desires.

The call can occur at any moment. It does not have to happen during a church service or a youth conference. It could happen while driving to work or grocery shopping. Remember, this is God. He can call anyone, at any time or place, as He sees fit. Physical location is not a prerequisite. A person does not even have to be a believer prior to receiving the call. Here is a true story to illustrate that.

Case Study: My Call to Missions.

I was sixteen years old, at the height of my professional sinning career. I had no desire to do right. I enjoyed being a sinner. After all, it was the only thing I was good at, and many people knew me as such. One day I was sitting on the living room floor watching a new television station called the Travel Channel. I started watching a show about Haiti. It was pretty interesting. Towards the end of the show, a voice shot through my body and said, "You are going there!" I jumped off the floor in fear, and looked around the house to see who said those words. To my amazement, I realized that I was in the house alone. After a few moments, I shook myself back to reality and forgot all about that moment. Six years later, I was born again and serving in Haiti on a one-month mission trip. During my time in Haiti, traveling from Port-au-Prince to Saint-Marc, that same voice said, "I told you so." All I could do was laugh. I had no idea that for the past six years I had been following God's voice.

Remember the call of God for missions can happen to anyone, anywhere, at any time. Just like the person in the story, it does not matter whether a person immediately responds or not. Eventually God will get His way. That is why everyone calls Him God.

If anyone suddenly finds him- or herself being called into missions, then the first suggestion would be to stay quiet and pray. Wait for God to confirm His calling. God will always confirm His calling. God will always confirm His Word. There is no room for lone rangers in the mission field. God does not speak contrary to His written Word. The Bible is clear: "In the mouth of two or three witnesses shall every word be established" (2 Corinthians 13:1). If God made the call, He will be faithful to confirm the call. God will often use people to confirm the call. The confirmation is not limited to laymen who work in the church. God will many times use the voice of strangers to confirm His call. It is often more than one person. Let there be no doubt that if God called a person to missions, God will send many people to confirm His call.

However, there is a conflict that coincides with the confirmation. Once the call is received and confirmed, there will be naysayers. Naysayers are people who try to discourage a person from pursuing God's call. These naysayers can be an overprotective parent, an unwilling spouse, or a skeptical friend. The most devious naysayers are pastors who are jealous or fearful of the person being called because it would mean fewer finances for his church. Yes, there are those pastors out there who do not want people giving to any other cause outside of his church. Such pastors will use threats, manipulation, and guilt in order to trick the person into not following missions. Such pastors will call young missionaries rebellious, immature, and unruly. Satan will use also the "man of God" to discourage a person who has a desire to be a missionary from becoming a missionary. Therefore, it is very important for a missionary to maintain an attitude of prayer. Listening to the voice of God, and reading His Word, will be the only solace during this challenging and confusing time. Patience is key.

In regards to patience, remember that this is only the first step of many more to come. How a person handles this step will determine future success in later steps to come. One thing that an emerging missionary should always pray for is patience. Patience will be needed when dealing with naysayers. It is inappropriate to react or respond in a manner that is contrary to the Word of God. Though it may feel good to lash out and speak evil, it is better to maintain a quiet mouth and allow God His time to do His work. No matter what naysayers may say or do, God will defend His call. He does not need any help.

Key Point to Remember

1. When God speaks, He always confirms His Word.

Chapter Two:

Grow Before You Go

The maturation process occurs from the time God makes the call until the time that God actually releases a missionary to go. This can take months to years. The longer the wait, the better success a missionary may experience. Many missionaries forgo the maturation process and jump straight into the mission field. The maturation process is often overlooked by the new missionary because there is a lot of excitement about the call. Once God calls a person into missions, there is a fire that is lit, that burns passionately out of control. If this passion is not put under subjection, the missionary will leave too soon, and burn out very quickly.

Remember, most young missionaries are extremely radical, and will do anything for their God. For this reason it is extremely important that young missionaries submit themselves to be accountable to spiritual authority. If a missionary is affiliated with a church then the missionary should be accountable to the local pastor. Keep in mind that a missionary who has no affiliation is deemed as a missionary without any form of accountability. Very often people will ask, "Who is your covering?" (Even though the use of the word "covering" is incorrect in its usage, the Bible does teach that leaders must be accountable to some type of spiritual authority.) This means that if a missionary is affiliated with a church, then the pastor should be the one to whom the missionary is accountable. This comes with a warning for pastors. A pastor who fails to watch over his missionary is the same as a father who lets his baby girl play with a loaded gun. It is that serious. A missionary cannot function properly unless he or she is in an accountable relationship.

If a missionary does not have any affiliation with a church or organization, then it is best for the missionary to assemble a group of strong Believers who will be able to speak into his or her life. A missionary cannot use his personal family as the ones responsible for maintaining spiritual accountability, because family members are less likely to confront certain issues. Neither can the missionary use someone from within the people group to whom he or she is ministering. The reason why this is not permitted is because generally the people group that is being reached are in general spiritual babies, and do not possess the knowledge or maturity to help a missionary. Also, this goes against the flow of spiritual authority. The Bible says, "The disciple is not above his master, nor the servant above his lord" (Matthew 10:24). The chain of authority comes from the top and goes downward, not from the bottom to the top.

A missionary must learn to lean on other members of the Body of Christ. Moreover, missionaries must surround themselves with people who are passionate for God, but have the wisdom of God as well. Remember, this is not a one-man show. Anyone who goes into the mission field alone is going to die alone. Therefore it is imperative that a missionary be connected to a body of Believers. The Bible teaches that there is safety in the multitude of counsel. This is a principle that a missionary must follow with all diligence. Having a set group of trusted people that can offer counsel is strategically important in the life of a missionary. There will be times in a missionary's career in which he or she will not be able to see things clearly, and will need an outside independent view of a trusted friend. Therefore, build and maintain Godly relationships with trusted people, and stay accountable to them.

Key Point to Remember

1. A Missionary must be accountible to a body of Christian Believers.

Test Your Knowledge

1. List three ways God may use to speak to you: _____

   _____

2. Which one does God use to speak to you?_____

   _____

What The Bible Says

1 Thessalonians 5:24

He who calls you is faithful, who also will do it.

New King James Version (NKJV)

Chapter Three:

Deal With Your Junk Before You Go

There are numerous motives behind why people choose to go serve on the mission field. As mentioned throughout this book, some go because they are called to go. However, there are those who decide to go because they are running away from a problem or situation in their life that they do not want to deal with. In missions, this called the "escapism."

Escapism in missionary language simply means that a person is using missions as a means of escape. This also coincides with the "fight or flight" theory in psychology. Instead of fighting or facing their situation, they choose to run away from their situation. Many people who use escapism normally are facing what they believe to be insurmountable circumstances or problems that they cannot seem to overcome in the moment, so they choose to take flight, instead of fight.

Here are a few examples of those who run:

Christian young people who come from troubled homes. It is more common today to hear about Christian youth who are growing up in homes where there are problems within their relationship with their parents. Many times, these problems can be attributed to two causes.

The first cause is the case in which the young person is a Christian and their parents are not. Unbelieving parents can lack the ability to empathize with their Christian child, and often times fail to understand the guiding principles behind their child's actions. The young Christian often feels alienated and misunderstood.

The second cause for problems within the home can be attributed to a breakdown in respect and communication between the Christian parent and the young Christian. Often times Christian parents can be overtly controlling, and often forget that their child is now an adult, capable of making their own decisions. The root causes for both of these problems are spiritual immaturity and insecurity. Young Christians need to learn how to follow basic Biblical principles on how to deal with problems within relationships. Running away is not always the best solution. However, if a young Christian is choosing to separate themselves from the situation and serve on the mission field in order to gain a broader view and then return to face the problem, this is noble. Sometimes by being around other positive relationships, an individual can see how to better fix their own relationships at home. This is the exception, not the rule.

Christian adults who are facing insurmountable financial problems. Many people seek the solace of the missions field because personal failure. These failures can be the loss of a job, business, home, bankruptcy, or a relationship. People who face these types of failures often feel embarrassed, and their self-esteem is low. People going through these types of problems view missions as a way to get away. Now understand that the problem is not necessarily the "getting away" part. The problem is the motive for getting away.

There are two main motives behind someone wanting to get away. The first motive is selfish in nature because the person wants to use missions as a means to rebuild his or her self-esteem. These types of people will go serve on the mission field to feel important. They thrive off of how the people that they are serving look up to them. It's all about ego. The second motive for why individuals use missions as a "getaway," is to get refocused. This is not as selfish as the first, but none-the-less not a good reason to serve. There are instances in which individuals would benefit from a short term stay on the mission field under the guidance of an experienced missionary. The main benefit would be a deeper knowledge of God, and how He cares for His people, regardless of their situation, or circumstance.

Christians who are facing a serious illness. When a Christian encounters a life threatening illness, they undergo a internal transformation. Many individuals after spending a lifetime selfishly seeking their own wellbeing, they begin to re-evaluate their priorities, and start focusing on things that have value. Though noble, this sentiment recedes in time. For some, once time and healing have taken place, the desire to do missions becomes an afterthought once again.

When looking at the motives behind why a person wants to serve on the mission field, it is always good to ask this question: Would this person have served in missions if they had never faced these problems? Generally, if these problems had not occurred, then missions would more than likely have not been even considered. Missions is NOT a last resort. It should never be used as an "if all else fails, become a missionary." Being a missionary is a LIFE LONG commitment. It should not be entered into unless there is a true calling by God Himself.

One thing is for certain; whatever problems a person is running from will eventually catch up to them on the mission field. Do not think for one minute that all because person is on the mission field that their problems will automatically disappear. Problems have a tendency to follow individuals on the mission field and it does affect the quality of the work, and the relationships built while serving.

Whatever emotional problems or character flaws a person had while in their home environment, will follow them to the mission field. The mission field will not magically turn a person with bad interpersonal communication skills into a person who is empathetic and kind, nor will it change a person with bad character into a person with good character. What will happen is that missions will tend to bring out the worst in those who have not dealt with their personal issues. So it would be a wise thing to check your motives before you go. Make sure that you are not running away from any unresolved problems. Do your best to mend and deal with every issue before leaving.

Key Points to Remember

1. Let your calling be true. Check your motives.

2. Never run away from your problems.

3. There is no problem too big for God. Trust Him.

Test Your Knowledge

1. What are three situations that people tend to run away from?

_____

_____

_____

_____

_____

What The Bible Says

Jeremiah 12:5

If you have run with the footmen,
and they have wearied you,
Then how can you contend with
horses?

New King James Version (NKJV)

Chapter Four:

Missionary Redefined

The word *missionary* has many different meanings and usages in our modern time. Different people and organizations have differing meanings of the word. For the sake of this book, a missionary is not a person who travels to many different places for a few days a year, or even a few days a month. Even though people who do such things may be doing missions work, that does not qualify them as a missionary.

A missionary is equivalent in function and purpose to the New Testament Apostles. There are no differences in function and purpose between the two. Understand that the title of missionary is not found in the modern English Bible. The Jesuits in 1598 are deemed to be the first persons to coin the words *mission* and *missionary*. These words are derived from the Latin *missionem* (nom. *missio),* meaning "the act of sending," or *mittere, mittat, mitto* meaning "to send," all of which are found in the Latin Vulgate translation of the Bible.

*"[E]t dicebat illis messis quidem multa operarii autem pauci rogate ergo Dominum messis ut **mittat** operarios in messem te ecce ego **mitto** vos sicut agnos inter lupos."* (Latin Vulgate, Luke 10:2-3)

*"Therefore said he unto them, The harvest truly is great, but the labourers are few: pray ye therefore the Lord of the harvest, that he would **send forth** labourers into his harvest. Go your ways: behold, I **send you forth** as lambs among wolves."* (King James Version, Luke 10:2-3)

However, when using the original Greek Scriptures, the word *send* in the same passage is *apostello* (Gr #649) meaning "to send out," or "to send forth." It has the same root meaning as the word *apostolos* from which we derive the word *apostle*. The meaning of the word *apostle* is "one sent forth." Both of these—*apostello* and *apostolos*—involve the act of being sent forth. Therefore, there is not a distinction between the two. *Apostello* is the action, while *apostolos* is a functional title. In short, if one were to translate the word *apostle* into English, the actual modern translation of the word *apostle* would be the word *missionary*.[1]

---

[1] C.T. Onions, *Oxford Dictionary of English Etymology* (New York: Oxford University Press, 1966), 240, 581.

One of the reasons behind why the word *apostle* was transliterated was to make sure that people would be able to distinguish the twelve Apostles from those who were not of the original twelve. However, in light of the meanings of these two words, whichever word a person chooses to use, whether it be *apostle* or *missionary*, is acceptable as long as its usage does not imply an equivalence in stature and posture to the original twelve Apostles.

Prior to the creation of the word *missionary*, the early church would differentiate the two titles by capitalization of the first letter. If one were to write or make mention of the original twelve Apostles, they were required to capitalize the first letter "A." If they were not of the original twelve, yet were actually serving as an apostle (missionary), then they were to write their title starting with a lower case "a."

Now that there is some understanding of the meaning of the word missionary (apostle), it is important to know the characteristics of a missionary (apostle). In agreement with the original twelve Apostles, the main definition of a missionary is one who is called into a land which is not his or her own for the sole purpose of reaching a people group with the Gospel of Jesus Christ. Even though there are those people who go to other lands to provide great humanitarian aid and social services, if they are not sharing the Gospel of Jesus Christ with others, then they are not considered missionaries.

In addition, true missionaries stay dedicated to the people group they are called to reach until death. It is never found in Scripture where an Apostle abandons his people group for another people group. Nor is it found that an Apostle will win a people group to Christ without providing lifelong follow-up and accountability. Many modern missionaries ignore the lifelong responsibility of providing follow-up care. Follow-up care is simply holding the people and their leaders accountable for what they teach and how they live. The minimum requirement that is vividly shown in Scripture is the writing of letters or epistles. There has to be some form of communication between the missionary and the people group won to the Lord. This means that the missionary will have to appoint leaders, and establish a means to communicate with that leader.

This implies that a missionary will need to invest months and years living among the people. This is an important realization because it takes time to win a people group. Once a people group is won, then they must be discipled. After they are discipled, then the missionary is responsible for appointing a leader from within that people group. This process could take years, or even a lifetime. Any individual who calls himself- or herself a missionary and has not lived among the people group is not a true missionary. Yes, such individuals may be doing missionary work, but they are not missionaries. Coming to this realization will help young missionaries prepare themselves for the long journey ahead.

There are many false notions that missionaries travel about the world, from place to place and country to country without any dedication or lifelong commitment to the people within that country. However in reality, people who travel in such a manner are what the Bible calls evangelists. Do not confuse the two. An evangelist is not a missionary. A missionary is not an evangelist. An evangelist may do missions work, but he is not limited to the lifelong commitment of a people group, or a geographical region. All missionaries are limited to a people group or a geographical region. Remember the Apostles were called to reach specific regions and people groups. Thus, missionaries are called to do the same.

Since missionaries are indeed apostles, then it is imperative that modern-day missionaries follow the traditions of the original twelve Apostles. In their apostolic tradition they divided themselves into groups, and then went into regions to share Christ. They never set foot in another Apostle's region to conduct ministry without first consulting the Apostle in charge of that region. This notion is expressed when Paul states, "Yea, so have I strived to preach the gospel, not where Christ was named, lest I should build upon another man's foundation" (Romans 15:20).

Even in modern times, many missionaries will not conduct ministry in a location where another missionary is working. It is imperative that young missionaries continue to follow this unwritten code of conduct. Doing so will avoid needless strife, arguments, and confusion. Paul gives a good example of this very same problem during his day when he stated, "Now this I say, that every one of you saith, I am of Paul; and I of Apollos; and I of Cephas; and I of Christ" (1 Corinthians 1:12). Paul makes this statement because many of the Christian Believers in Corinth were confused and divided because Apostles Apollos and Peter were individually coming into the region at differing times teaching salvation and baptism.

The problem was not with their teachings. The problem was their lack of communication with each other, and with the various Believers in Corinth. When Apostle Apollos showed up, he ministered to one group. When the Apostle Peter showed up, he ministered to a different group. Neither of the two groups was connected. Thus when Paul arrives, he finds the various groups divided and confused. This leads Paul to begin the task of correcting the error and unifying the Believers.

If a missionary finds himself- or herself working in a region where a missionary already exist, then it is important to build a rapport with that missionary, and try to seek approval prior to conducting ministry.

To demonstrate how the original Apostles operated, here is a map of the regions and people groups to which the Apostles were assigned.

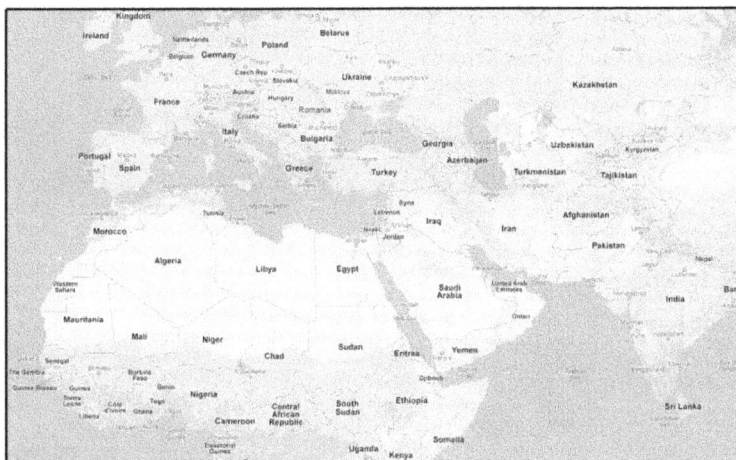

Beside the name of each Apostle are the countries in which they traveled.[2]

Andrew: Georgia and Bulgaria
Bartholomew: India
James, Son of Alphaeus: Jerusalem
James: Judea
John: Samaria, Asia
Matthew: Ethiopians, Macedonians, Persians
Simon the Zealot: Egypt
Peter: Turkey, Jordan, Italy, Asia
Philip: Greece, Syria, Turkey
Paul: Turkey, Greece, Rome
Thadaeus (Jude): Syria, Mesopotamia, Libya
Thomas: Tehran, India

---

[2] Catholic Encyclopedia. Vol. 5. (New York: Robert Appleton Company, 1908)

Chapter Five:

Learning Another Language

Learning the language of the people is imperative. Utmost priority and diligence should be given to achieving this effort. Language is the only way to properly communicate the Gospel. Whether the Gospel is presented in verbal form or written form, the use of language cannot be avoided and must be learned. Learning the language of the people is a salvation issue. If a non-believer is unable to hear and understand the Gospel message, then that person runs the risk of dying without knowing Jesus Christ. This means that person runs the risk of spending eternity in a Devil's Hell.

This is a serious issue. Many missionaries forgo language learning because it can be a difficult task. Many missionaries are too lazy to dedicate themselves and exercise their brains to learn a language. How is it that God can call someone to reach a people group in a foreign land, and yet not give that person the ability to learn the language? If a missionary has been called by God, then that missionary will be equipped by God. God will not send someone into any situation without preparation and equipping. God is a God of order. Understand that God has given everyone a measure of faith. That means that God has planted inside every person certain capabilities. However, it is up to the individual to recognize that fact. The problem is that many missionaries negate the fact that they have been enabled, equipped, and empowered to learn the language of the people. Satan will use many tactics to prevent a missionary from coming to the realization that he or she truly does possess the power to learn the language. The goal of Satan is to make the missionary as ineffective as possible. If he can trick a missionary into not learning a language, then he can resort to using his master plan of confusion when the Gospel is being presented. Yes. This is true. Satan is the author of confusion. If a missionary cannot clearly present the Gospel to an individual, then Satan can and will come in and confuse what the missionary has said.

Another trick that Satan uses to con missionaries into not learning a language is good old pride. That's right: Satan will build up a person's pride to convince them not to learn the language. There are many missionaries out there who, because of their pride, do not wish to learn, or even attempt to speak in a native language. They tend to wrestle with thoughts such as:

"I will sound like a fool."

"They will laugh at me."

"I do not want to embarrass myself."

"I do not want to say the wrong things."

"English is a superior language."

"Their language sounds stupid, and I will not drop to their level."

All of these thoughts originate from Satan himself. Just as God planted the ability to learn language inside every missionary, Satan has also planted thoughts inside of every missionary to help them not learn the language. Many of those who are attacked with pride are older missionaries. The reason older missionaries are attacked with pride is because generally, older missionaries come from backgrounds in which they are accomplished individuals. Generally, they are highly educated and astute, and have held respected positions. The fear of losing the respect of others is the key to their weakness. Individuals of such caliber struggle with presenting themselves as buffoons. This is said because learning a language initially makes a person feel like a buffoon. It is like going back to infancy to acquire language for the first time. It is extremely embarrassing for some, and can often turn missionaries away from language learning.

The best way to overcome and break through this barrier is for the missionary to be reminded that they have been enabled, equipped, and empowered by God Himself. God gave the gift of the Holy Spirit to man. With this gift comes the power to do any job, the tools to do any job, and the ability to learn any job. Remember, a missionary must take a step of faith in order to see the Mighty Hand of God at work. In this case, the step of faith is for the missionary to start learning the language. Allow the Holy Spirit to do His Work. He promised that He would bring things back to memory. Forgetfulness of words in a language is no big deal to God. God will be faithful to fulfill His part of the deal. Here is a story to illustrate this idea.

Case Study: My Supernatural Language Acquisition.

Many years ago, I went to a Saturday night prayer meeting at my local church. People from different denominations were all praying for God to revive our city and save lost souls. I began to pray in English. I noticed that after about fifteen minutes of praying that the sanctuary became energized, and people started praying aloud, and shouting praises. I tuned them all out and continued to pray. As I was praying, the pastor tapped me on the shoulder and said, "Boy, what type of language are you speaking? Sounds like some of that 'Po le vue France' stuff." I was amazed. He heard me speaking in a language that I had not learned. After the service, he asked me, "Why do you think God gave you that language?" I told him that I didn't know why it happened; it had never happened before. "Well," he said, "it sounded like some type of Frenchy stuff." A year later, as I was preparing to go

---

to Haiti for the first time, a missionary gave me a book and a cassette with phrases that I needed to learn before I arrived. Lo and behold, the language of the Haitian people was French Creole. It sounded exactly the same as the language I had spoken during that prayer meeting. From that day on, I never had that particular experience again. However, I dedicated myself to learning French Creole. The time I invested really paid off. A few days after I arrived in Haiti, I was given the opportunity to present the Gospel. I began to speak French Creole. At the end of my message, 85 people received Jesus Christ as their Savior.

Key Point to Remember

1. Learn the language of the people you are going to serve.

1. What is the native language of the people you are called to reach?

_____

_____

_____

_____

_____

What The Bible Says

Acts 2:8

And how is it that we hear, each in our own language in which we were born?

New King James Version (NKJV)

Chapter Six:

$\mathcal{M}$*issions and* *Money*

A missionary needs finances in order to work on the mission field. There are many different perspectives about how a missionary should go about obtaining finances. One thing is for certain: money is needed in order to preach the Gospel.

There are those missionaries who have an overly optimistic view of their financial future. Almost everyone going into missions has this optimistic view that finances will come out of nowhere with very little effort put forth. They think that they do not have to lift a finger to get money; it will just show up. This overly optimistic view will lead one over a ledge of disappointment. This view is promoted by ministry leaders who teach the notion that if God wants something to be done, then God will provide finances for that work to be accomplished.

Every missionary believes that God has called them to do a great work; hence every missionary believes that God will provide for their specific work. However, a sad reality arises when after months and years of hoping and waiting, God does not miraculously provide the finances. Yes, there will be those who claim they received money from out-of-the-blue, but for the majority of missionaries, this does not happen.

Some effort on the part of the missionary must be made.

Unless a missionary decides to work for a professional missions agency, then most likely a missionary will need to raise some type of financial support. This is a very humbling experience. Sometimes, it can even be a humiliating experience. Many people who felt called to missions have changed their minds after realizing that they have to kill their pride and ask for financial help.

There are five ways missionaries and missions agencies generate income. The money that they raise is to be used to sustain the missionary and the missionary's ministry.

The first most common method is asking friends and family for financial support. If the missionary comes from a less than privileged background, then that support will be short-lived. Generally, poor families cannot afford to support a family member as a missionary.

The second most commonly used method is to be supported by a local church. However, this too can be short-lived if the church supporting the missionary has a small congregation. Generally, small churches are unable to sustain the long-term efforts of a missionary.

The third most common method is sending out support letters to other churches. This is like shooting a rabbit in the dark. Most churches will not respond to such solicitations. Nowadays, churches want to support those that they know. So that requires a missionary to visit other churches. This method is the most useful, but also the most time-consuming and costly. It can take up to two years for a church to feel confident enough to support a missionary long-term.

The fourth method is simply pay-your-way. This means that the missionary and/or his or her spouse work part-time or full-time to earn the money that they need to sustain themselves.

The fifth method used to generate financial support is the implementation of a short-term summer outreach program. A short-term summer outreach is when a group comes to visit a missionary or missions agency for a few days out of the summer and volunteer their time to help the ministry. Many times these groups will pay a nominal fee to participate. These fees in turn are used by the missionary to sustain themselves and their ministry.

Be aware that there are missionaries out there who use missions as a means to generate wealth. They do this by charging groups excessive fees which are above and beyond what is reasonable.

Therefore, it is important for a missionary to avoid the appearance of evil by maintaining open records. Allow people to see how much items cost, and how their money was spent. Always keep receipts, and ask vendors for receipts. Have a third party entity review all financial documents for inconsistencies and errors.

Now that it is understood how missionaries generate income, let us explore some of the different attitudes and philosophies about work, finances, and missions. Even though many missionaries have their own points of view about this topic, this next section will focus on the main perspectives that are held by most if not all missionaries.

There are two general perspectives on finances and missions. One perspective is that missionaries should be 100% devoted to God, focusing only on the task and believing God to supply finances. This means living 100% off donations, and not having any outside employment to earn money.

This type of teaching will lead a missionary down a road of unrealized dreams, and unnecessary suffering. This manner of teaching breeds laziness, and a lackadaisical attitude about having a good honest work ethic. Missionaries who follow this teaching often live on mission compounds where there is a communal living arrangement, in which they pay fees to an organization for food, housing, and education.

The second perspective is that missionaries should have employment and work for the things that they need. This is called bi-vocational missions. This means that missionaries either work in the country in which they are called to serve, or they work part-time in America for short seasons, and do missions on a part-time basis. However this too poses a problem. It promotes the notion of self-sufficiency, and lessens the need to walk by faith. Let's face it: if people can do it on their own, then why do they need God's help? Many missionaries are self-made missionaries who have the practical knowledge and work ethic to go out and earn the money they need for their missions work. This usually limits their work to small projects. It is rare that missionaries who live by this principle have large ministries. Normally, in order to have a large ministry, it takes the support of outsiders who donate to the work at hand.

The Biblical perspective would be to work to earn money, while at the same time trusting God to provide for the needs that may arise. The Bible illustrates that Jesus was a carpenter; Paul had a part-time job as a tent maker, and Peter owned a shipping company. All these individuals were self-employed, with jobs where they had complete control of when and where they worked. However, as their ministries grew, there was a noticeable transition from working to support themselves to living off the support they received from other Believers.

One of the most prominent examples of this is illustrated by Paul and the Philippian church. Prior to winning the Philippian church, Paul supported his ministry by building tents. However, after winning a Philippian lady by the name of Lydia to the Lord, she and the other Philippian Believers started funding Paul's missionary journeys. So who was Lydia? Lydia was a wealthy Philippian. The Philippians were some of the wealthiest people of their time because their region was a trade hub for different nations. They were the ones who funded most of Paul's missionary journeys.

Therefore, it is extremely important that missionaries walk in a balanced frame of mind. Yes, a missionary should work; however, a missionary also must learn to live by faith, allowing God to provide. Remember what the Scriptures state: "Not by might, nor by power, but by My Spirit, says the Lord" (Zechariah 4:6).

A missionary also must guard his or her finances at all times. A missionary is entrusted with finances. Those finances belong to God, and the missionary is just a steward. With this, there is a warning also. Beware of wolves in sheep's clothing. There are those people who will befriend a missionary with the hopes of gaining their trust. Once trust is won, a knife in the back soon follows. These types of people exploit the weaknesses of the missionary. The motivation behind these wolves is always money and power. Here is a true story to explain this point.

> ### Case Study: A friend tells his story of betrayal.
>
> *After seven years of service on the mission field, I decided to allow a close friend from another ministry to help me run things. I placed him on my board of directors, and he began to assume numerous work duties. After a while, I felt that I could trust him to run things, so I went back home for nine months. Upon my return, I was told that I was no longer in charge and that my long-time friend had removed me from the board and put his family on the board. When I went to talk to my so-called friend, he said, "Your services are no longer needed. I've got this ministry now." There was nothing I could do. I lost my home, vehicles, money, and everything that I worked for. I began to look for the people that I used to help, and none of them wanted to talk with me. Then one person who I never thought would be my friend told me, "Brother, the people in this country will follow the money. They don't care about you, your work, the ministry, or the guy that took over. They only care about the money. And as soon as the money is gone, they all will be gone."*

There is this underlying thought some people think that missions does not generate good income, and that it bleeds resources from a church. That is definitely far from the truth. If done properly, missions can generate more revenue in a month than most churches generate in a year. As discussed earlier, there are people out there who will use missions as a way to generate wealth. However, there are also pastors who are just as guilty. They will use missions as a means to generate extra money during offering time because they know people will give towards a good cause. These types of pastors will take up offerings under the guise of giving to missions, but in reality, they are reallocating the funds for other things. It is up to the donor to investigate and communicate directly with the missionary to inquire about how much money a church is giving.

One of the warning signs to look for in a church that is falsely raising money for missions is that the church will never open its financial records for public review. Another sign would be that the church limits contact with the missionary; the pastor acts as a go-between and discourages a donor from communicating directly with the missionary.

Many times the ones who have concerns about where the money is going are the donors. However, there will be times when the missionary should be concerned as well. Missionaries should always be on the lookout for "red flags." Red flags include the ones previously stated, plus one major additional red flag to look out for. The major red flag that a missionary should look for is the church's failure to give you a donor list. Churches may avoid doing this for various reasons, so it is imperative that a missionary take the time to ask questions and investigate how much money is being raised, and where the money is going. Here is a story to illustrate this point.

Case Study: A church that robbed its own missionary.

During a summer missions program, an assistant pastor and another church leader came to visit me in Mexico. During their visit, they were taking numerous videos and traveling throughout the region enjoying the sights.

During one meeting we began to discuss finances. I explained to them that we do not receive a lot of money. We have been surviving off of $300 a month for the past five years. The assistant pastor was outraged. He stated, "Brother, you need more money. How in the world can you properly operate this ministry with only $300 a month? I am going to go back to talk to the senior pastor, and I am going to raise funds for your ministry." So the assistant pastor took the video footage and made a huge presentation to the church congregation, asking people to give to our missions program. As I was watching the broadcast, I became excited. I was thinking that we finally have the help and support that we have so desperately needed and been waiting for.

After a few days passed, an elder called me and told me that after the presentation, the church raised

---

> *about $6,000 and that we should be receiving that money very soon. Well, after a few weeks passed, I realized that our ministry had not received the donation yet, so I called the co-pastor to inquire about the donation. She was shocked that I knew about the donation. Then she proceeded to inform me that the donation was not meant for our missions ministry; it was going to be used for something else. My heart dropped, because they raised that money using the video that showed our faces, names, and ministry work. I did not think that it was fair that people gave under the guise that they were giving to our missions ministry, when in fact they were not. It is sad that many people even until this day do not know that we never received the money.*

All missionaries who study this book need to be above reproach. Try to make sure all financials are open to the public, or at least to those who give support. Do not be greedy for money. Avoid the temptation of money. Put the needs of others first.

Chapter Seven:

$\mathcal{P}$ lanning With Purpose

Some of the unnecessary hardships that a missionary faces are due to a lack of planning. As the saying goes, "If you fail to plan, you are planning to fail." This is 100% true. A missionary must sit down and take the time to plan his or her missionary journey from beginning to end. This chapter will teach missionaries a foolproof method for successfully embarking on a missionary journey. In addition, this chapter will include a missions planning journal. This journal will help missionaries develop a realistic outlook on the journey before they leave.

As stated before, failure to plan is one of the most common errors of a young, ambitious missionary. In general, when God tells a missionary to go serve a people group, land, or country, there is often excitement about the destination without thinking about the journey. Here is a key insight: The farther the destination, the longer the journey; the longer the journey, the more planning is needed.

Do not expect things to just fall into place all the time. Yes, God will provide, but a missionary also has a big responsibility to plan. Take time to read the following story. This story will provide vital clues on how to plan.

Case Study: A Missionary's failure to plan

There was a young missionary who was called to India. He was fresh out of high school. He had no training, no money, and no support. He stated that he wanted to go to India and live there for the rest of his life. However, he did not have any contacts there. He could not speak the language. He was totally ignorant of the culture. He did not even know which city he would go to or how to get around that city. So, I asked him, "What is the first thing you are going to do when the plane lands in India? Where are you going to go? How are you going to get there? If something happens, how are you going to make it back home?" He simply replied, "I will trust God to provide and guide me."

Needless to say, this missionary never accomplished his dream of living in India. In this story, the missionary was asked three big questions. These questions are summarized in the following three topics:

1. Getting there:

2. While you are there:

3. Returning from there:

This next section of this book is a list of questions based on these three topics. It is highly recommended that every missionary be able to answer all of these questions in detail before traveling abroad.

I Getting there:

1. To what country are you called to go?

_____

2. In what community are you going to live?

_____

3. How much does it cost to get there?

_____

4. What documents do you need to get there and stay there?

_____

5. Have you ever been there?

_____

6. Do you know someone there?

_____

② *While you are there:*

1. Where are you going to live?

   _____

2. How much will it cost to live there?

   _____

3. How long will you stay there?

   _____

4. What are you going to do while you are there?

   _____

5. If you get sick, where will you go?

   _____

6. How will you get around?

   _____

7. What language do they speak, and can you speak
   the language?

   _____

8. How will you receive money?

_____

9. Who will send you the money?

_____

③ **Returning from there:**

1. How will you return to America?

_____

2. Where will you go?

_____

3. Who is going to pick you up from the airport?

_____

4. Where are you going to live?

_____

5. How are you going to eat?

_____

6. Do you have transportation?

_____

7. Do you have enough money for food and shelter?

_____

To achieve effective planning, young missionaries should take the information above, and prioritize in reverse order. In other words, start with the last category first, and make that your number one priority. Therefore, your first priority should be:

3 Returning from there:

2 While you are there:

1 Getting there:

Generally for independent missionaries, the biggest problems generally occur upon returning from a missionary journey. This is especially true if you have a family traveling with you. Here is an account from a missionary based on his true personal experience:

Case Study: My Failure to plan.

I remember my first year living abroad as a missionary. It was awesome to see how God took care of me and my family. I remember how I mapped out every gas stop and rest stop along the way. I remember all the effort I spent making sure that we had a safe place to live upon our arrival. A year later, it was time to return home. We packed up our things, loaded the truck, and began the long drive back home. When we made it back to America, I had made arrangements to stay at a guest house for a few days. The owner of the guest house asked me, "Where are you guys going to stay once you arrive back in your home town?" That was a question that shot fear throughout my very being. With all the planning that I did, I failed to make plans for where we were going to live. I spent a few days from that point calling people I knew in my home town, and no one could assist me with housing. I was extremely discouraged. Then I got a call from a friend who said we could stay with them. It was not the best place in the world. It was a house deep in the country. When we arrived, they took us to a room in the very back of the house. It was their wash room. They gave us a mattress to

---

put on the floor, and that is where we lived for a short time. It was winter time and extremely cold in that room because there was no heat there. My wife cried, and I swore to her that we would never go through this again. So from that point on, I started planning in reverse prior to doing anything else. This method has kept my family safe for years, and I believe it will keep any missionary safe if they will follow it.

What The Bible Says

Proverbs 15:22

Without counsel, plans go awry,
But in the multitude of counselors
they are established.

New King James Version (NKJV)

Chapter Eight:

Satan's Debt Scheme

The call of missions sometimes comes at the most inopportune times. While in the midst of pursuing the American dream, people suddenly find themselves called into the mission field. This pursuit of the American dream has a side effect which teaches people to live outside of their means, buying things that they cannot afford, and often times getting into severe debt to pay for those things. However, when a person becomes a missionary, they have to learn how to live within their means. This implies not buying things they cannot afford, and not incurring debt. It seems as though many people have been brainwashed into an American way of thinking that causes people not to be frugal, prudent, and save money. Instead, some people tend to spend, borrow, and spend some more.

What is even more bizarre is the phenomenon of many young missionaries who are severely in debt because they made the mistake of funding their mission trips with credit cards, thus at some future point terminating their call to missions. Remember, if a person is in debt, then that person is bound to eventually take a regular job to pay off those debts.

In a sense, debt is a tool that is often used by Satan to stop potential missionaries from becoming missionaries. His scheme is across the board. He wants to entrap as many people as possible. The more he entraps, the less likely it is that people will enter the mission field. In short, he is trying to put everyone in debt to stop them from going on the mission field or supporting missionaries from home. He knows that if people are in debt, they are less likely to become missionaries because they would feel obligated to pay off their debts first. Moreover, since 80% of Americans are in debt, that severely decreases the possibility of someone being sent. This can be avoided if young people would read this book and avoid debt altogether. If God calls someone into missions, and that person is in debt, it is recommended that he or she use the following strategy to get out of debt.

STEPS TO SUCCESS

Step One: Live on a budget.

If you are going to be a missionary, you will have to learn to live on a budget. A budget is very difficult to use, especially if your income is sporadic. So what I would recommend is that you make a list of essential expenses. Essential expenses are those things that are essential for you to survive.

The basic essentials are food and shelter. Since no one can survive without food or shelter, it is important that you calculate a realistic amount each month that you and your family will need. In my personal experience, I generally budget $15 per person per day. (This could be more or less depending on food prices.) Your housing expense should be whatever is written on your rental or housing contract.

Make envelopes for each expense, and fill each envelope with its designated amount as your support comes in. Do not spend more than what is in the envelope.

So here is how it would work. Let's say that your food budget is $500 per month, and your housing is $300 per month. You would fill the food budget first, and once you have reached the designated amount, then you would move on to filling the housing envelope. If there are more expenses, prioritize them by necessity in descending order. Here is an example of how your budget should look:

Family Budget

Housing.................$300
Food......................$500
Transportation.....$200
Utilities $50
Cell phone.............$40
Clothing................$100
Entertainment.......$30

Step Two: Avoid credit card debt.

Avoid getting into debt...especially credit card debt. You do not need credit cards for "emergencies" or to reserve hotel rooms, rental cars, or airplane tickets. Get a Visa check card. If you are afraid you might have an emergency, open a savings account and save money for emergencies!

Step Three: Avoid car loans.

Car loans have to be repaid, and it is very difficult to pay your car loan if you are a bazillion miles away in the middle of a jungle. Moreover, you will not be able to take a car out of the country if you still owe money on it. If you need a car, go buy a cheap car, under $2,000, and pay cash for it.

Step Four: Avoid student loans.

If you cannot afford a particular college, GO TO A CHEAPER COLLEGE. If you are already in debt, you may qualify for a deferment, but you will eventually have to leave the mission field in order to pay off that debt.

So how does a missionary spend his or her money? Many people give to missionaries, but they do not know how their donations are being spent.

Remember, when a missionary is receiving financial support, those finances are not only to cover ministry expenses, but also to cover living expenses. Remember the Bible says, "Even so hath the Lord ordained that they which preach the gospel should live of the gospel." (1 Corinthians 9:14.) This means that those who preach make their living off the donations they receive from preaching the gospel. So, if a missionary receives a donation, do not be surprised if that donation is spent on other things.

The primary goal of the missionary as declared in 1 Timothy 3:5 is to take care of his family first, then the ministry. Therefore the missionary must be allowed to spend the donations as needed. However, if a missionary states that the money is for a certain project, then the law—and Godly stewardship—requires that that money must be used for that project.

Key Point to Remember

1. The American dream, is only a dream. Missions is the reality.

1. What are the three things a
   missionary must avoid?

   _____

2. In your budget, which item would
   be your first priorty, and why?

   _____

What The Bible Says

Ecclesiastes 10:19

A feast is made for laughter,
And wine makes merry;
But money answers everything.

New King James Version (NKJV)

Chapter Nine:

*B*reaking *Ethnicity Barriers*

A missionary's ethnicity can be a barrier. It is extremely important that a missionary is not ignorant of the fact that prejudice continues to exist in the world. Yes, there are people in foreign lands who will prejudge a missionary based on his or her ethnicity. Ethnicity may play a role in which country a missionary should serve. There are even situations where ethnicity may determine how much financial support a missionary will receive.

According to the Center for World Mission, less than 1% of missionaries are African- American. Within that small group, there is a consensus that African-American missionaries do not receive as much financial support as Caucasian missionaries. In some aspects of missions, there is still an underlying thought that white missionaries do a better job at missions than blacks. However, it is also a fact that the majority of black churches are not huge financial supporters of foreign missions because black churches are more concerned with fighting social issues within their own communities.

As for racism abroad, there is very little open racism. If anyone enters the mission field thinking that every Christian is color-blind, they are mistaken. Racism abroad tends to affect Caucasians more than African-Americans. However, there are other issues that should be discussed more deeply.

In the past, Christianity has allowed racial superiority to permeate doctrine, thus allowing teachings which propagate one race to be superior over another. The biggest error of Christianity was when people mixed colonization with Christianity. As European countries began to colonize the world, they also brought with them their distorted views of Christianity. Many times these views justified segregation and apartheid. European Christians commonly misinterpreted Scripture to justify their actions to the colonized ingenious populace. Such teaching focused more on race and ethnicity than the love that Christ has for all people.

Many such teachings were based on this Scripture: "Cursed be to Ham. For he shall be a servant of servants to all his brothers." They would interpret this to mean that Ham, the Biblical father of the African race, would serve the non-African people. The Scriptures actually state:

"And He said, Cursed be Canaan; a servant of servants shall he be unto his brethren." (Genesis 9:25.)

Ham had three other sons who were not cursed, and they were: Egypt, Ethiopia, and Libya. It will never be seen in Scripture where God preferred one race over another. However, such teachings in the past had a devastating effect on the mission field. This devastating effect is a phenomenon, specifically coined for this book, called "interethnic racism." (racism against one's own race).

Case Study: My experience with racial preference.

I remember traveling to Haiti for the first time. Our team had to travel across the ocean in a small boat to get to an island. There were three blacks and five whites on our team. Once our boat had docked, we all grabbed our own luggage and proceeded to walk down the road. As we were walking, villagers came and carried the luggage of the white missionaries, but did not even offer to come carry the luggage of the black members of the team. We noticed that during our entire time in the country, the Haitians were more hospitable to the white missionaries than to the black missionaries.

This story is not saying that this only happens to blacks. Racism can happen to anyone regardless of skin color. Many Caucasians tend to face the realities of racism when working in certain areas of Africa and Latin America. The deciding factor is the country in which the missionary works, and that country's views about ethnicity.

1. What was the result of mixing colonization with Christianity?

_____

_____

_____

_____

_____

What The Bible Says

Galatians 3:28

There is neither Jew nor Greek, there is neither slave nor free, there is neither male nor female; for you are all one in Christ Jesus.

New King James Version (NKJV)

Chapter Ten:
$\mathcal{D}$efeating Gender Stereotypes

Gender can be a huge obstacle, whether visible or invisible, in missions. There seems to be a large presence of female missionaries as compared to male missionaries. Most statistics tend to validate this point of view. In 2001, there were 5.52 million Christian workers in the world. 60% of those were female. Even though the female presence tends to be larger in numbers, male missionaries tend to be more respected, and tend to receive more support. This is partly due to Biblical teachings on the woman's role within the leadership structure of the church. This is not to say that women should be discriminated against. A female missionary can hold the title of missionary and can function freely as long as her role does not place her in a position of spiritual authority over a man. Many traditional mission agencies reject the notion of females holding positions of spiritual authority in a church.

The trials that a female missionary will encounter are on a totally different level than those of a male missionary. Female missionaries are sometimes viewed as outcasts or inadequate. Most agencies do not respect the ideas presented by female missionaries. Many times female missionaries are ignored or given only menial work to do. Women who go against the flow are often viewed as rebellious, and thus their support is cut off.

The best way to work as a female missionary is to be 100% submitted to God's Word. No matter what the social trends are at the time, the Word of God endures forever. People can be whatever the Bible says they can be, and they can do whatever the Bible says they can do. Do not allow personal views to cloud the truth of God's Word. Remember, the call is from God, and the work belongs to God. If someone has been called by God to do God's work, then God will make sure all obstacles are removed. It makes no difference if a person is male or female. God will be faithful to those who submit to His Word. This means that a person has to walk in Biblical humility. Walking in humility and putting the needs of others first are signs of submission to God's Word. Many people would rather fight and defend their "rights" and their pride, but the Word of God clearly states that justice belongs to God, and He will make sure no injustice goes unpunished. This means that if there is an issue with gender bias, then the goal is not to be confrontational. Be submissive to God's Word, and allow God to do His Work. Do not be stopped by obstacles, nor be an obstacle to others.

Chapter Eleven:

$\mathcal{D}$efying Age Bias

Right now, there is a growing trend of retired persons entering the mission field. Because they are retired, they are entitled to special benefits abroad. In addition, it should be noted that most retired persons receive a pension, which means that they are more financially stable. For this reason, older retired persons serving on the mission field do not encounter all the stressors that younger missionaries encounter. The first question a person should ask any missionary is how they are supported.

Many older missionaries give the false impression that they are supported financially by numerous churches in order to give a false impression of success. Understand that there is something of a stigma placed on missionaries who do not appear to be living by faith. Many independent missionaries tend to look down on those missionaries who work for agencies that offer salaries and benefits. Why? The answer is related to the culture of missions. Within the culture of missions is the general belief that everyone who serves must depend on God for all their needs. Those missionaries who have received the most financial support are often viewed as being more blessed than the others. In other words, the more a missionary has, the more people think he is succeeding. Thus there is this pressure for older missionaries not to disclose that they may be receiving a pension or Social Security funds.

In the case of young missionaries, they have different problems altogether. Young missionaries are often perceived as untried, untested, unseasoned, immature, unstable, inexperienced, and mostly flat broke. Younger missionaries have a more difficult time breaking past these perceptions, because for the most part, they are true! Moreover, it simply takes time to win the confidence and the support of others.

A few keys that will help you win the confidence of others:

1. *Be confident.*

2. *Make a plan and stick to it.*

3. *Keep your word.*

4. *Keep in touch with people you meet.*

5. *Share from your heart, not from your empty pockets.*

6. *Stand on your own feet, asking for as little as possible.*

7. *Stay committed to your vision, and do not change your mind.*

In addition to these, there are three other things a missionary can do to break through this barrier. The first is to serve more within their local church or ministry. When people get to know a young missionary's passion and work ethic, they will be more confident in the missionary's abilities to perform on the field.

Secondly, the young missionary can pursue higher education in a field related to his missions work. A well-educated and well-prepared young person will always be preferred over a young person with no preparation. Education is key. Nobody wants to support an ignorant missionary.

The third and final way to break through this barrier is marriage—though this is NOT the best way. Many young missionaries will marry just to give the appearance of stability. Why do they do that? This is due to the fact that many people view a married person as stable and mature because of the responsibilities that are required to maintain a marriage. The logic is this: If a person can take care of his wife, then he will be able to take care of the ministry. This is a Biblical principle that many young missionaries use to gain support. Be aware, however, that those who marry for the wrong reasons always end up in divorce. The mission field is not a place for two people to start a marriage, unless they have both been called and confirmed for the work.

1. What seven things can you do to gain the confidence of others?

_____

_____

_____

_____

_____

What The Bible Says

1 Peter 5:6

Therefore humble yourselves under the mighty hand of God, that He may exalt you in due time...

New King James Version (NKJV)

62

Chapter Twelve:

$\mathcal{P}$utting Your Emotions in Check

All new missionaries should be aware of the "honeymoon phase" in missions. It is in effect a romanticized view of missions in which everything is seen as perfect. New missionaries arriving for the first time in a new country tend to experience the honeymoon phase during the first six months of their tour. The honeymoon phase is typically when a missionary is captivated by the culture and sees things through rose-colored glasses. The missionary is oblivious to the social woes and other issues within the culture. After the first six months, the honeymoon phase is normally over, and what is left is a disheartened missionary who now has to deal with the reality that the job is not easy, there are a lot of problems, and it will take a lot of work. People who only come for short-term trips less than six months never experience this phase.

The best way to ease the pain of the end of the honeymoon phase is by constantly remembering that the exuberant feelings during the first six months are not real. Spend time talking to people about laws and customs. Spend the first six months learning as much as possible, and do not do any type of work. NO EVANGELISM. NO MINISTRY. DO NOTHING!

Just spend the first six months learning. Resist the urge to conduct ministry. Remember, it takes time to learn what the real needs are. Take time to learn what the real needs are, and take the time to learn how to best meet those needs.

Many young missionaries are gung-ho, and they go in with guns blazing, kicking down doors, knocking over sacred cows, and stepping on toes. Then when the people are not receptive to their message, the young missionaries are left bewildered, discouraged, and dismayed, and tend to return home defeated with no desire to return to missions. This can be avoided if a missionary learns not to rush, and spends the first six months learning the people.

If there is already a more experienced leader who has been in the country for a longer amount of time, most new missionaries feel the temptation to be highly opinionated. Avoid strife. Be quiet. New missionaries often struggle with feeling like they know more than the established missionary. They often feel that the experienced missionary is slow, passive, inactive, docile, etc. Remember that if a new missionary has been in the country for less than six months, then more than likely the new missionary is too ignorant and blind to see things clearly. For the next six months, it is best to be quiet submit, follow orders, and just LISTEN.

Many times new missionaries are not aware of the laws. They begin to do things that may be legal in their home country, but may be illegal in the country to which they are called.

This is especially true in Latin American countries. Many ministries come into these countries and hold evangelistic outreaches in community parks. One would think that such acts of free speech would be deemed legal; however, it is illegal to do so without government approval. Although many authorities will turn a blind eye to foreigners who break the law, such is not the case for those who are nationals. So remember, learn the laws. Be above reproach.

Once the honeymoon phase is over, now it is time to deal with loneliness, depression, and dismay. One of the most unexpected problems that a missionary may face on the mission field is loneliness. It is important that a missionary be mentally prepared for the probable and sudden realization that "you are not in Kansas anymore!" Loneliness can manifest in many different ways. It usually starts with, "Man, I wish I could get a cheeseburger!" or "I miss hearing my own language." Loneliness affects ALL missionaries, especially those who travel alone. There is no surefire way to avoid it. One of the things that can help ease the pain is by making the people YOUR people. In other words, become deeply immersed in the culture. Make friends. Do not be afraid of being vulnerable. Do not be afraid to show weaknesses. Weaknesses can be the strongest witness. Unlike the westernized church theology of "BE YE PERFECT," just remember that no one is perfect, nor can a missionary ever be perfect. Everyone has frailties and weaknesses. God will use those things to build a bond with others. JUST BE REAL! The following saying is a quote from a missionary:

"Be real with yourself, and be real with others. Remember, God ain't afraid of REAL, and neither should you."

Missionaries who fail to deal with their loneliness will find themselves in depression. Once depression sets in, dismay will soon follow, and then hope will be lost. The missionary must then be immediately removed from the mission field.

Key Point to Remember

1. Do not be a know-it-all. Be quiet and learn.

Chapter Thirteen:

$\mathcal{B}$e Unifiers and Not Dividers

Missionaries must be unifiers and not dividers. It is important always to work with various churches and promote unity in the Body of Christ. This can be challenging because many churches want exclusivity, meaning that they do not want to share their work with others.

Be aware that there is a rivalry among different mission organizations and church denominations. It is sad to state, but it is true. If a person chooses to work for one denomination or one organization, then that will more than likely limit the chance of receiving support from an organization or church that is nonaffiliated. For example, a Pentecostal missionary is less likely to receive support from a Baptist church. A missionary with YWAM (Youth With A Mission) is not likely to receive financial support from the IMB (International Missions Board). This is not to say that it will not happen; however it is less likely to happen. For this reason, it is important that missionaries try to stay neutral as much as possible. Do not side with one denomination over another. Missions is the function of the entire Body of Christ. Therefore it is imperative that we as missionaries encourage all Christians everywhere to be equal participants.

There will be organizations and churches that will demand loyalty. Be loyal, but be loyal with an open heart. Do not allow control and manipulation to limit the ability to be mobile. Being mobile simply means having the freedom to work with various organizations or church denominations without fear of reprisal. Always be neutral. Stay out of politics. Make everyone feel that they are valued. Resist the temptation to talk against or side with anyone. Always speak well of others, and always promote the John 17 philosophy.

The John 17 philosophy is simple to understand. People will know that Jesus Christ exists by the love Christians have for one another. The goal of the missionary is to bring unity to the Body of Christ. Therefore, love and unity are key to winning the world for Jesus Christ. Without a unified effort from all churches and organizations, a missionary is powerless. Missionaries need the united support and efforts of the Body in order to be successful in their mission. There is no other way. Those who think they can do it on their own will experience absolute failure.

Chapter Fourteen:

*C*onfronting *The* *Fear of Death*

The final issue that must be discussed is death. Missionaries must learn to conquer the real possibility of death. With the advent of certain types of prosperity teachings, people have become content to love the pleasures of this present life. With such teachings that focus more on personal growth and financial gain, many people find themselves entangled with the cares of this world rather than focusing on their eternal reward that is soon to come. The physical gains that this world has to offer are temporary at best.

The primary problem in the mission field is the fact that missionaries are teaching a more materialistic version of Christianity. This is the version of Christianity that teaches that people can have the good life on earth. Even though God does bless His people, the focus of the Christian walk should not be on material wealth.

Whenever the attainment of material wealth becomes more important than the Cross of Christ, the message of true salvation is of no effect. If people are receiving Christ only to receive material wealth, then they have not received Christ at all. Christ came to save mankind from the punishment of Hell and make possible a relationship with God. The sins of mankind only lead to Hell. Without the Cross, Hell is the only reward a sinful man can hope to receive. Salvation to receive material gain absolutely does not exist.

When a person loses their focus on the cross of Christ, the resulting consequence is a strong attachment to this world, and to the things of this world. This breeds a brand of "Christians" who are less likely to stand up for their beliefs. Christians who are afraid to defend the truth of the Gospel will not die for Jesus.

When Christians are afraid to die, change never comes to a society. During the first 300 years of Christian history, Christians who had wealth were not afraid to stand up for the truth, even if it meant death. The early Christians suffered horrible fates at the hands of ruthless rulers. Through their persistence and courage in facing death, change eventually came to their society. The reason why missionaries do not see the type of revivals and change within non-Christian countries is because Christians are afraid to die for what they believe in. They would rather enjoy the little comfort that they currently have than to suffer and die. Missionaries must get back to the true teachings of the Gospel message. New converts must be taught to focus on their eternal reward, and not the riches this world has to offer. Missionaries must teach new converts to share their faith even if that means death.

Missionaries have to be retrained in the first-century version of Christianity. There needs to be a revival of missionaries who are not afraid of death. The world needs missionaries who will stand against injustice, and be willing to die for speaking the truth. Rather than shy away from those who threaten to kill, missionaries should trust in their God. They should focus on their eternal reward, and speak the truth of Christ. Millions of people who serve false gods will die in service to their false gods. Yet Christian missionaries are still a bit squeamish about the notion of dying for the cause of Christ. Even though they know He is real, the word "death" is the proverbial line in the sand for many missionaries. A missionary who fears death does not deserve the right to be called a missionary. Being a missionary is not for the cowardly. Being a missionary is not for the weak-willed nor faint of heart. Being a missionary is for those who KNOW their God, and are willing to die for their God.

Key Point to Remember

1. There is nothing on this earth that can compare to what is waiting for us in Glory!

Test Your Knowledge

1. Why do some Christians fear
   death?

   _____

   _____

   _____

   _____

   _____

What The Bible Says

Philippians 4:6-7

Be anxious for nothing, but in
everything by prayer and supplication,
with thanksgiving, let your requests be
made known to God; and the peace of
God, which surpasses all understanding,
will guard your hearts and minds
through Christ Jesus.

New King James Version (NKJV)

Epilogue

The fact that you have taken the time to read this book shows that you are serious about doing missions work the right way. It is our belief that we had to go through these things so the generations that will come after us will not have to fall into the same traps. Use this book as a spiritual road map to help you avoid some of the common mistakes many new missionaries make. The benefit is that by avoiding some of these pitfalls, you can enjoy a greater measure of success on the mission field.

Many times God will allow you to go through challenging situations for the sole purpose of teaching you how to teach others how to get through it. Just imagine how many people tried to cross the jungles of Africa and failed. Their failures were the roadmaps to success. If you so happen to fail, please do not look at it as a waste. Look at it as an opportunity to teach others how to avoid the same mistake. Eventually your failures, trials, and tribulations will become a roadmap that others can use to guide themselves through uncharted territory.

After serving more than ten years on the mission field, I will tell you that God has never failed to provide for our family and our missions work. Yes, we endured some minor hardships, but our hardships are what enabled us to write this book. We want you to learn from our mistakes, and try to do things better than we did. You have our roadmap to help guide you. Now go forth and win the world for Jesus!

What The Bible Says

Proverbs 3:5-6

Trust in the Lord with all your heart, And lean not on your own understanding; In all your ways acknowledge Him, And He shall direct your paths.

New King James Version (NKJV)

Bibliography

Bible. Latin. Vulgate 1956. Romae: Typis Societatis S. Joannis Evang., 1956, c 1927.

Catholic Encyclopedia, The, Volume V Copyright © 1909 by Robert Appleton Company, Online Edition Copyright © 2003 by K. Knight Nihil Obstat, May 1, 1909. Remy Lafort, Censor Imprimatur. +John M. Farley, Archbishop of New York.

Catholic Encyclopedia, The, Volume VII Copyright © 1910 by Robert Appleton Company, Online Edition Copyright © 2003 by K. Knight Nihil Obstat, June 1, 1910. Remy Lafort, S.T.D., Censor Imprimatur. John Cardinal Farley, Archbishop of New York.

Jones, Robert C. *Meet the Apostles: Biblical and Legendary Accounts.* (Createspace, 2010).

Kirby, Peter. "Hippolytus of Rome." Early Christian Writings. 2006. 2 Feb. 2006.

Oxford Dictionary of English Etymology, The. Onions, C. T. 1873-1965., Oxford University Press [1967, 1966].

Your Missionary Journal

It is important for every missionary to keep a journal. As a part of your missionary development, you should keep a daily record of your experiences. The best way to record your experience is by dividing your journal into three sections.

The first section of your journal should record your pre-trip expectations, feelings, and beliefs. Try to explain what your expectations are prior to your trip. Then explain how you feel prior to your trip. Finally explain what you believe God will do during this trip. Try to be as detailed as possible.

The second section of your journal should record your daily feelings and emotions from the time you arrive until the moment you leave. Try to see if God is meeting your pre-trip expectations. Record as much details as possible.

The third section of your journal should record your post trip realities. Try to answer how you feel after the trip. Did God meet your expectations? Explain yourself as detailed as possible.

Once you finish your journal, put it away for 30 days. Then come back and read what you wrote. Try to answer the following: How do you feel about what you wrote? Do you currently feel the same, or is there a change? Send an email to: *raf@omiinternational.org* and share your feelings.

Pre-trip Journal Entry

Mid-trip Journal Entry

Post-trip Journal Entry